POSTMORTEM OF A CANDY HEART
Tall Tales From My Feather Bed

Book Design by Kamryn McKenna
Photography by Will Shellhorn
Styling by Ryan Spataro

Printed in the United States of America
First edition, 2024

ISBN: 979-8-8692-9546-0

POSTMORTEM OF A CANDY HEART
Tall Tales From My Feather Bed

By Amelia

Contents

This is a work of fiction. However, any similarity to actual persons, living or dead, is entirely intentional.

Heroine

I am nothing if not a Shakespearean heroine:
One thousand lovers and one million disappointments
Letting fire burn and cauldron bubble,
Reducing letters to ash like bridges.
I understand (as we all do)
That some matches are made in heaven
While others delight in the flames.

I understand (as we all do)
That the hands of heroines are seldom unbloodied
We take the fall, we absorb the violence.
A broken heart is right twice a day
And like a clock it ticks with quiet brilliance,
So when the damned spots and the flames rinse off
We are left with nothing but melodrama
Loving the pursuit of elusive selves
Who speak their speech as they were scripted to
Sans thoughts, sans teeth, sans everything.

A hero once told me to get to a nunnery
And I called him my lord
Said I thought nothing, that I was his forlorn spaniel.
My cauldron bubbled over with disdain
But I delighted in the flames,
Grateful to finally understand (as we all do)

That heroines alone are allowed the immortal joy
Of fighting a little,
The achingly gorgeous act of fending for yourself
Of holding your own fragmented skeleton in your own
bloody hands.

Ferment our bodies for eternity, please
Bury us in fennel
In rosemary and pansies,
Shrouded in a legacy for the generations.
We love existing this way:
Carrying the scent of daisies and violence,
Sleeping peacefully underneath a cover of divine horror
That we finally understand
(We all do.)

Thwarted Showgirl

It's fine, I'm fine!
I'm in my prime!
It's just a tale of callous stealth,
Hiding but sublime:

A thwarted showgirl
A card shark prince
A quiet-zealous shadow love
Ruling a sundown supper kingdom,
Piloting a hellbound dove.

After many bitter pills
And grotesque martini thrills,
We afterpartied our way home to Eden.
With God's hand in the sky
And daybreak light in our eyes,
We embraced the luck of the innocents:
Something we didn't know we needed
Righteous advice that was heeded,
Though it dampened every nightclub show.

Quiet zealous shadow love,
Cardshark prince, God above
Give to me what mercy never could.

You might not be mine, but you're mine
Alright?

A garden lies in wait for the slyly divine,
Nocturnal players in a furtive Eden night.
I'm fine.
I'm in my prime!
It's fine.

For The Boys

I didn't realize I'd shot myself in the foot until I saw the blood
But when I looked around, it was everywhere.
The horror of the gruesome scene omitted,
It burgeoned on beautiful
Liquid relics shimmering in the bathroom sink.

It began with an absence.
Evening brought a cavity where he had been
And I was left alone and out of sight
Tucked beneath his bed like a vial of opium, or a monster.
Feathery twilight covered the walls with sugar
As I waited for him to come back
And sell me stories with his calligraphic voice
Feed me the world in digestible aggregates,
Placed in my mouth like grapes I was lucky to receive.

Though for the first time, there underneath his mattress
I began to feel tiny palpitations of my own knowledge,
Tethers to truths he could never weather.
I felt my yearning for frenzied autonomy
Taking the shape of a flintlock pistol
That must have been in my pocket all along.
The thing was delicate and confounding
An ivory body, coral veins punctuated with diamonds
I would never play with guns, I swore to myself.
And yet I was in his room, wasn't I?
Down the meandering staircase on tiptoe all the way

To the Great Hall and its feasting congregation
I flung open the door, bejeweled weapon in hand, and
there they were:
Securely embodied as my mind will never get the chance to be,
Encrusting a table like priceless gems
Savoring self-aggrandizing glory,
Chewed to the bone and discarded.
Questions danced in their searching eyes, I just knew it:
Why are you here, lovely poser?
Who was hiding you, wasn't me!
And why do you look so distraught?
Is it because you play with guns like they are toys,
Men like they are boys?
What do you expect, then?

What do I expect?
I expect a pardon!
They are all jewels on my crown,
My cause for defiant reverence.
They are my convicts to catch
In the throes of their virility
My procession of hungry kings
Whose days I will fill with alienation
Like mortar between bricks.
I will fabricate bespoke Stockholm syndrome for them

As they did for me,
Beautifully tailor-made for the one forced to wear it.

So I stood there, weapon in lithe hand
Position assumed, ready to draw blood from all those
Who pinned a paper doll on top of me.
The gun went off with a crack.
But it was my blood that was everywhere
It was my foot with a hole through it
It was me.
Always, it was me.
And I didn't realize it until I saw the blood.

Let it be known
That now I am privy, and always pithy
With this to say:
I know how it feels to gather dust under someone's bed,
To know that he's sucking marrow off the bone
While you're the one living with the consequences.

nk
ATM
Diet oke

Freudian Slip

Did I just call you Jesus?
Oh my God, sorry, Freudian slip!
I must have confused you with someone else,
Someone who reminds me a lot of you
With hands like two halves of a prayer
And a pirate ship smile I could dock all my dreams on.
Did I say I was out of commission,
That my face antithesizes how you look at me?
I swear I didn't mean it!
What I meant to say is that I'm an artless idealogue,
So diligently dreamy
That I run into walls, poles, the corners of everything
Until there are cuts and bruises on my legs,
Little tokens of my radical belief in the mythical.
I pretend to ignore them, willing water to be wine
And your time to live eternally in my back pocket
As I make charmless quips like a newly verbal mime.

nwc
Chameleon
SPA·NAIL

The World's Great Lovers

All the world's great fighters are dead,
But the world's great lovers remain
Holding desert sun in our hands
And sink water in our mouths.

The world's great lovers are conservators
Of the resources that feed our children's precious minds,
The very things that cultivate unbridled innovation
And make us victorious in each war effort.
Yet we are bonafide pacifists, we swear!

The world's great lovers
Are often convinced that a violent end is near
To be brought upon us
By the monks that wander arid horizons,
Attire mimicking the landscape.
Their peace appears threatening
And though we have never been burned or withheld
We search for any excuse to defend our paranoia,
Justifying it as fear in shaky black ink
Scrawled out over an agitated sky.

When I first arrived here,
I looked in my side pocket and realized
I had brought a pen to a gunfight
So I accepted my fate as a great lover
And stopped consuming altogether.

I have not even brushed my teeth since
Rinsing my mouth instead with stubborn panic,
Each drop of endangered water
Dissolving on my tongue as if I were the desert itself.
I let the apathy overtake me.

The world's great fighters have departed,
Bones turned to fossils and fossils turned to oil.
They have been replaced by people of no rebellion
Just sun and sink water.
As for me, I've been holding the living lovers close
And the dead fighters closer for a long time now.

On the walk home
I made up my mind that this is where I want to live:
In an impossible wasteland with impossible melodies echoing
As my teeth rot under the black ink sky.

Nostradamus

You foreteller, you!
I say to myself
As I watch a tiny Lamborghini circle the front yard
Around and around me in orbit.
I emanate light from the chaise lounge,
Offering myself up in convergent rays of warmth:
Here's some sisters (for collusion)
And here's a swimming pool (full of delusion,
To splash in while I drink a martini).
In the foggy emptiness of the glass
The olive pits make patterns of the future and the past
Rendering what has been like a secret fresco,
What will be like a vellum gilded with prophecy.

He met me on New Year's
(But I met him much earlier)
So I already knew his reservoir eyes
My hot pink sneakers
How together we stood colossal and blurry.
There was only one ending.
He picked me up on East 79th
To show me around his world,
All the places that compose an unlikely childhood:
Symphony of beauty, gild, feigned generosity.
I chose not to see it for what it was
As we sipped Aperol on his roof
Bubbles like tiny window lights decorating the orange sky.

I plotted the beginning.
I plotted the end.
I plotted the waterproof chaise lounge
(And the 4 pm dirty martini)
I plotted the daughters, and what little remained
I left up to fate.

But today I am locked in a cosmic chess match against myself
A self of fire and fear, such drive to fight
She would have been terrified by a lawn this green
By colors and circumstances this vivid.
But that girl was a foreteller, too
So she knew
Her marriage announcement would grace the New York Times
And she would be the giver of three lucky lives.
She decided she did not feel like fighting.

That harrowing peace will remain for forty years
Until I am sealed up and moved on,
Through an aisle into afternoon light.
I see them in the graveyard, sunglasses up on their heads
Paralyzed with relief that I am dead
My girls, sending me into the beyond
Reading out the eulogy with even tone:
Our mother did not feel like fighting.
She wore her lucky like a parka
Through each languid day,

The magnetic armor of denial.
We wear ours like a class ring
Sparkling under the crushing weight of good fortune.
Car doors slam and sunglasses go down over dry eyes
Instead of blessing me there in the backseat
After I have braved an unspeakable departure
They collude, searching in vain for an escape plan
From what they know they will always be.

The sun dips down beneath the pool
And she jumps on my legs, startling me.
What's in your glass? she asks,
Eyes as glittery as a bygone New Year's Eve.
It's the future, I almost say
I'm reading it as I have been forever
Since I was burrowed in a stagnant cosmic sea,
Dreaming up the contours of my life.

Let's take a rest, I whisper instead, and hold her to my chest
Maybe if we don't move the stars won't shift
And the sky won't turn
And time won't pass, predictions remaining unfulfilled.
Maybe this life spent in shadow I've had to myself,
Three delicate clock hands in orbit around me
Until time buckles under my weight.

Troilus

Troilus waits:
He is silent, he is overrated.
He doesn't speak because
He has nothing to say.
Well I have a lot to say
And I'm going to say it
Brush my teeth with rusted marrow,
And misperceive my force.

Troilus weighs his options:
The many sides of heaven
And there's just so much to choose from,
He wanted us to know.
But he picked bloodlust,
And again he would do it
Old Glory comes up for no air
And it seldom doubts itself.

On Troilus ticks,
He's a clock that thinks it's well-adjusted
But the gears are rusted
He can't tell time for anything.
Yet there's something more than nothing here
A damp cloth, a savior complex
Hand on heart, eyes to Jesus
And wring the blood back out.

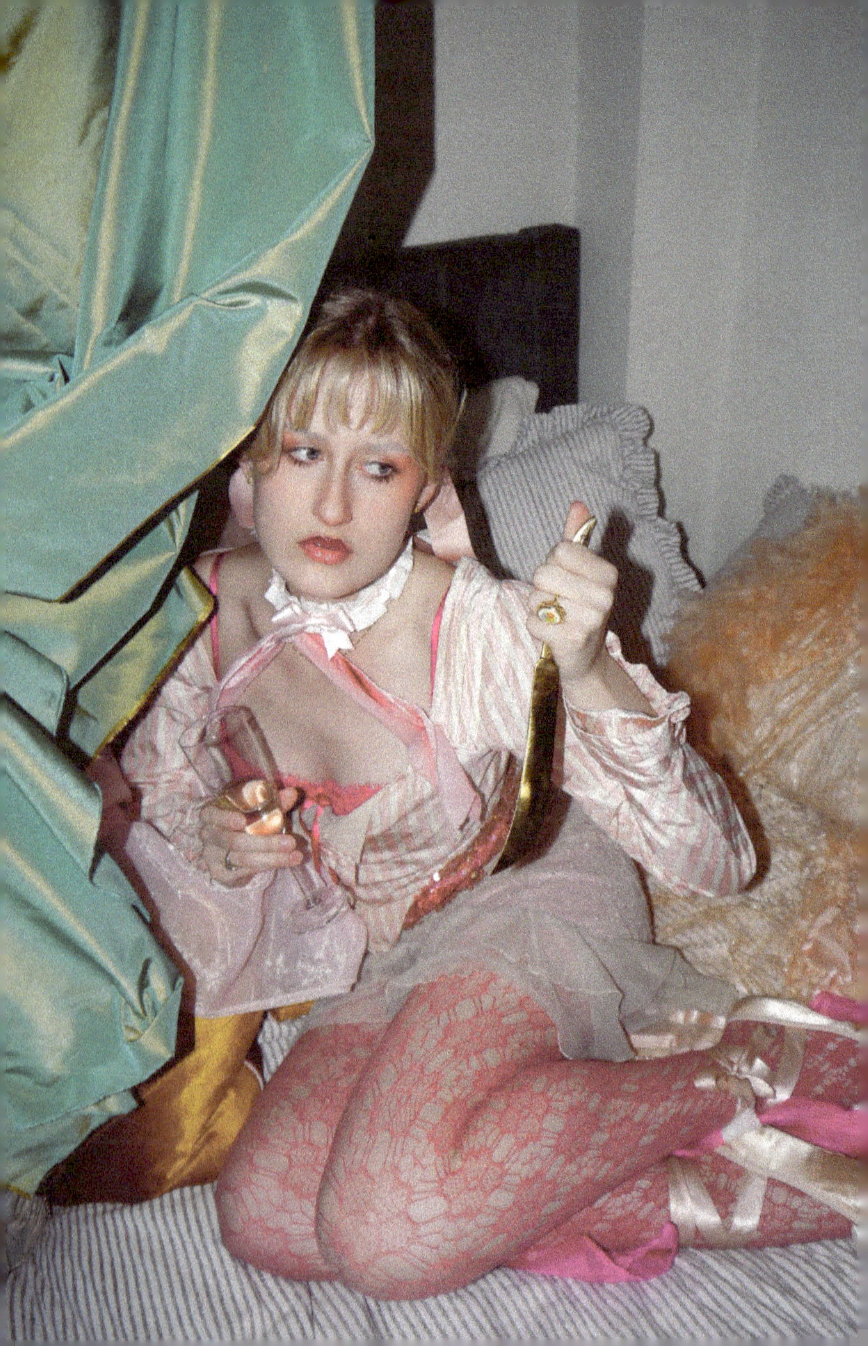

In the course of an afternoon,
I became a prophet
Because I arranged a marriage
That was strangely filled with love.
Cressida kisses his canine mouth
She's a tramp but he's a dog who's feral
Plainclothes cop with sterile morals
And she wants to get caught.

Postmortem

Is this a postmortem?
I'm unsure even as I stare blankly at the cold metal table.
I want to cut it open so badly,
Let this being robbed of life bleed out on the tip of my knife
Revealing some clue like jinxed treasure
Within scattered stories I cannot piece together.
I raise the blade but find myself unable
To cut into something so precious, so right
Made of flesh and venom and haunted nights.
Should I do it?

The dream you dreamt was my dream too:
As a storm reanimated the sky
A dull knock, a look up
My reflection in the windowpane
Staring back with glassy deference, question quiet as a tomb:
Should I do it?
With unsteady fingers I unlatched the door
And there you were, crystalline and weary
Guided by heavenly hand to my porch.
Where's your coat! I exclaimed, *You're wet from the rain!*
Come inside where the women are, the world will soon freeze over
My sister's making tea of bitterness and four leaf clovers
This isn't what I meant when I said you could come over
But you've etched epics in the floors now
And we all hope you're not leaving

You make it look like you're not suffering
Or bewitching us, or breathing.

Eyes akin to mine that watch me always
Spied through little holes in the wall, breath bated
As your fingers traced folds of wrinkled trepidation
Never wandering past the edge
Of what you sought with presumptuous defeat.
But it was never not bound to happen,
And I was never not bound by another's insistence
Even when it left an unused word on my tongue and a
bite on my neck
What did you say? you asked
Nothing, I said, and rolled over.

I'm entitled to my narrative
I think now, looking backwards
Into the void of what was before, after, after that again
Echoes of who I was before I dreamed of looking in
But like an ill-fitting sweater my story is tangled in a semantic war
Too bound up in yours, growing sparser as I pull the threads
Until I am left frostbitten in the morgue's sterile cold.

Is this a postmortem? I need to know now
The knife is up and I swear I will do it
Though I'm adhered forever to a sticky goodbye:
You've been here in this life, I pleaded, *Do visit in another*

I'll be here, drinking bitter luck every morning with my mother
Barely breathing through the days,
Indignance in my palms and forever grief on my fingertips
As they trace the sweet, bewildering improbable.

My floors retain the letters of a deathless tale
As years pass by and squeamish shame prevails
The knife is left to rust in fevered solitude.
Until another night, another storm, another knock at the door
Another translucent caller drops his bags on the floor.
Rattled breath is all that has become of my voice
Softly cooing against the rain beneath roiling clouds above:
Say nothing for a minute,
I want to tell you a thing or two about posthumous love.

A Toast

Glory, glory to the masses
Who constructed all the mothers
Of inferiority, paper, scissors
To love them fiercely but to never be enough.

Glory, glory to my origin story
Because mother, you couldn't hurt me
Steel and stuffing and fear and sweat
Is how you made me
To be yours
To see as you see.

Glory, glory to surpassing the unmatchable
Gracefully counting sheep,
Awake while in your sleep
Knowing no worship could ever serve your soul
To you mourning your body
To trips to the potty
To books you read to me with spines of gold.

Mother, mother, glory to incompetency
To blessing us, every one
Daughters and sons
Who were loved by their inferior mothers
With the ferocity of a fever dream
To reasoning with reason
To playing with words and flattening seasons

SLICE   PIE
EESE
PPERONI $2.50 $14.99
CHICKEN BUFFALO $3.50 $17.99
CHICKEN B.B.Q $3.50 $17.99
CHICKEN BACON RANCH $3.50 $17.99
WHITE RICOTTA $3.50 $17.99
PPERONI W/ SAUSAGE $3.50 $17.99
SAUSAGE $2.99 $14.99
PEPPERONI BACON $3.50 $17.99
PINEAPPLE $2.99 $14.99
CHILLI CHICKEN $3.50 $17.99
MUSHROOM W/ OLIVE $3.50 $17.99
SLICE   PIE
13. HAWAIIAN $3.50 $17.99
14. PEPPERONI MUSHROOM $3.50 $17.99
15. JALAPENO W/ PEPPERONI $3.50 $17.99
16. PEPPERONI MUSHROOM $3.50 $17.99
17. MUSHROOM $2.99 $14.99
18. MARGHERITA PIZZA $3.50 $17.99
19. VEGETABLE $3.50 $17.99
20. BEEF PATTY $3.00
21. PEPPERONI ROLL $3.50
22. BR $2.00
23. C $3.00
24.
25. $2.50
1 CHEESE SLICES
$1.50
2 CHEESE SLICES WITH
1 SODA CAN OR WATER
$3.99
2 PEPPERONI SLICES WITH
1 SODA CAN OR WATER
$5.75
2 HOT DOGS WITH
1 SODA CAN OR WATER
$5.50
WHITE RICOTTA $17.99
CHICKEN BUFFALO $17.99
BRO
BEE
COOKIES
COMBO #1
2 CHEESE SLICES
WITH 1 SODA
CAN OR WATER
$3.99
COMBO
2 PEPPERONI SL
WITH 1 SODA
CAN OR WATER
$5.7
50

Into pages of a book you bound yourself.

Glory, mother, mother!
You couldn't hurt me
One of many, many of one
Who you are is what I'll be
When the masses put inside me something burning
Some glory mother's story no one told.

On East 12th

I almost wasn't able to tell you what I saw today
Because I walked right over them at first
But then I heard fluttering like the whispering of secrets
So I turned around and there they were,
Hundreds of pages of the New York Times
Scattered all over the concrete on East 12th.

The president was dead,
He had been shot in Dallas.
Dizzy fear sped up through the decades
And through layers of years I felt it all:
Time holding its breath
The end of American myth
The beginning of lawless scavenging for identity,
Cold panic of a tetherless nation.

I tried to ration with irrational facts:
The pages were yellowed.
The last century had been draped in a flag and replaced.
Yet there was the news, at my feet
Bloody words that once traveled across highways as if
they were veins,
The only thing keeping fifty disparate parts together
Besides a dream that could end with the pop of a gun.

I wish my great grandparents could have seen what I saw
today: Heaven.

It's a place where the great family dynasties are anonymous
And the regattas go on all night long,
Sails twirling and collapsing from the winds of avoided tragedy.
I saw where the killers go
I saw a play
I saw a ballet.

I tell you this because I want you to know
Life's a bitch and then you're shot in a Lincoln Continental
In a city that's not yours
On East 12th.

And yet the regattas sail on
The New York Times puts ink to paper
The ballerinas spin.

ACKNOWLEDGMENTS

For my parents and for Avi. I love you.

Deepest gratitude to Brian Pawlikowski and Brandon Cohen for their feedback and support. Thank you to NYC Poetry Creatives for the space to write and workshop.

Will, Ryan, Kamryn - this book is yours as it is mine. None of it is possible without you. I am forever grateful for your encouragement, creativity, and dedication to this project.

@ameliaagorman
@boytoyry
@kamrynmckenna
@willshellhorn

* 9 7 9 8 8 6 9 2 9 5 4 6 0 *